Bilingual Picture Dictionaries

My First Book of

Hindi

Words

by Katy R. Kudela

Translator: Translations.com

apple
सेब
(seb)

CAPSTONE PRESS
a capstone imprint

Table of Contents

How to Use This Dictionary

This book is full of useful words in both Hindi and English. The English word appears first, followed by the Hindi word. Look below each Hindi word for help to sound it out. Try reading the words aloud.

Topic Heading in English

Topic Heading in Hindi

Word in English
Word in Hindi
(pronunciation)

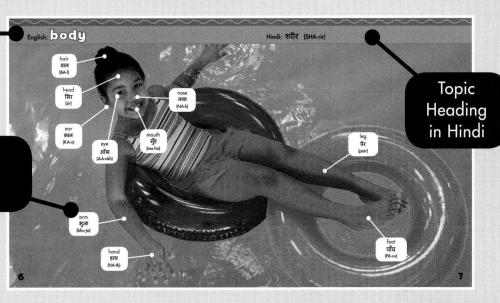

English: **body**

Hindi: शरीर (SHA-rir)

hair
बाल
(BA-l)

head
सिर
(sir)

ear
कान
(KA-n)

eye
आँख
(AA-nkh)

nose
नाक
(NA-k)

mouth
मुँह
(mu-ha)

arm
भुजा
(bhu-ja)

hand
हाथ
(HA-th)

leg
पैर
(pair)

foot
पाँव
(PA-nv)

6

7

Notes about the Hindi Language

Hindi is written in the Devanagari alphabet and draws vocabulary from Sanskrit. Hindi has 14 vowels and 33 consonants.

Devanagari is written from left to right, but capital letters are not used.

The Hindi language easily adopts foreign words. English words like "car," "bus," and "computer," are written in Devanagari script but are pronounced like English.

In Hindi, the number six is pronounced (chhah). The extra "h" means the "ch" sound should be pronounced while breathing out heavily.

In Hindi, some words have no emphasis placed on syllables. These pronunciations are shown without capital letters.

uncle
चाचा
(CHA-cha)

cousin
चचेरे भाई-बहन
(cha-chere BHAI-be-han)

mother
माता
(MA-ta)

aunt
चाची
(CHA-chi)

baby
बच्चा
(ba-CHCHA)

4

grandmother
दादी
(DA-di)

father
पिता
(pi-TA)

grandfather
दादा
(DA-da)

brother
भाई
(BHAI)

sister
बहन
(be-han)

5

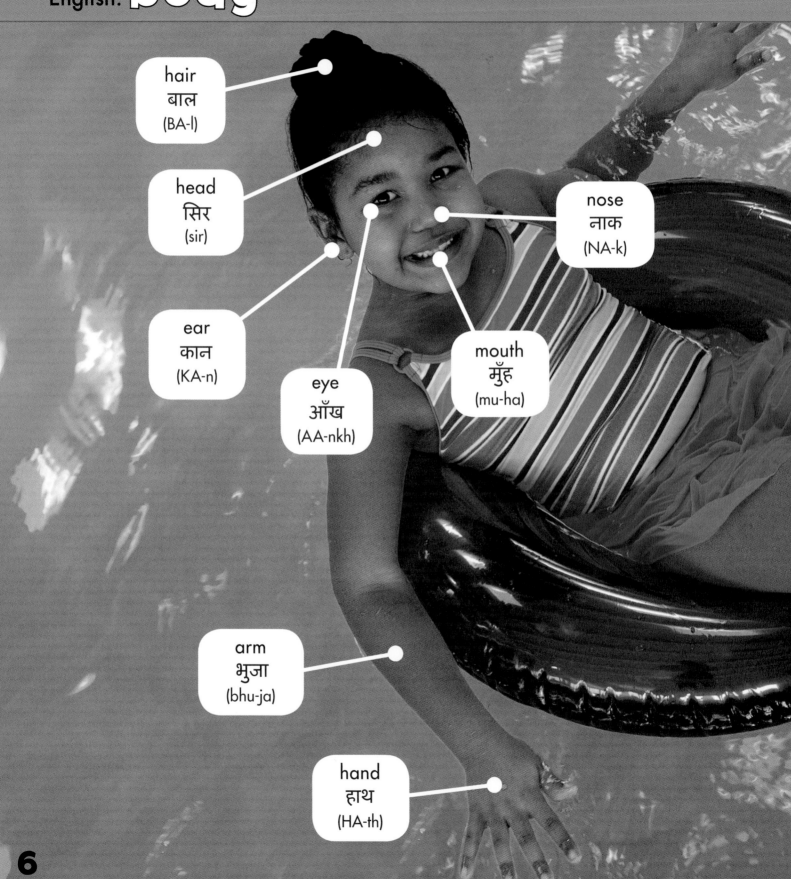

hair
बाल
(BA-l)

head
सिर
(sir)

ear
कान
(KA-n)

eye
आँख
(AA-nkh)

nose
नाक
(NA-k)

mouth
मुँह
(mu-ha)

arm
भुजा
(bhu-ja)

hand
हाथ
(HA-th)

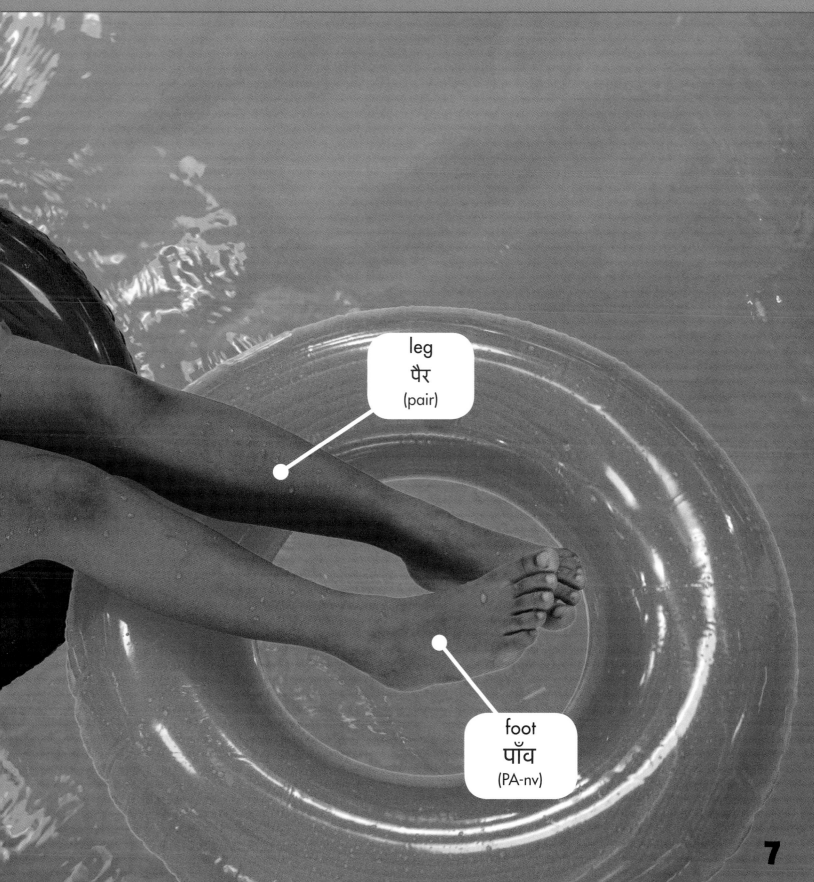

leg
पैर
(pair)

foot
पाँव
(PA-nv)

pajamas
पजामा
(pa-JA-MA)

coat
कोट
(KOHT)

shorts
शॉर्ट्स
(shorts)

boot
बूट
(boot)

8

shoe
जूता
(joo-TA)

hat
टोपा
(TO-pa)

pants
पैंट
(pants)

sock
मोजा
(mo-JA)

dress
पोशाक
(po-SHA-ka)

shirt
शर्ट
(SHURT)

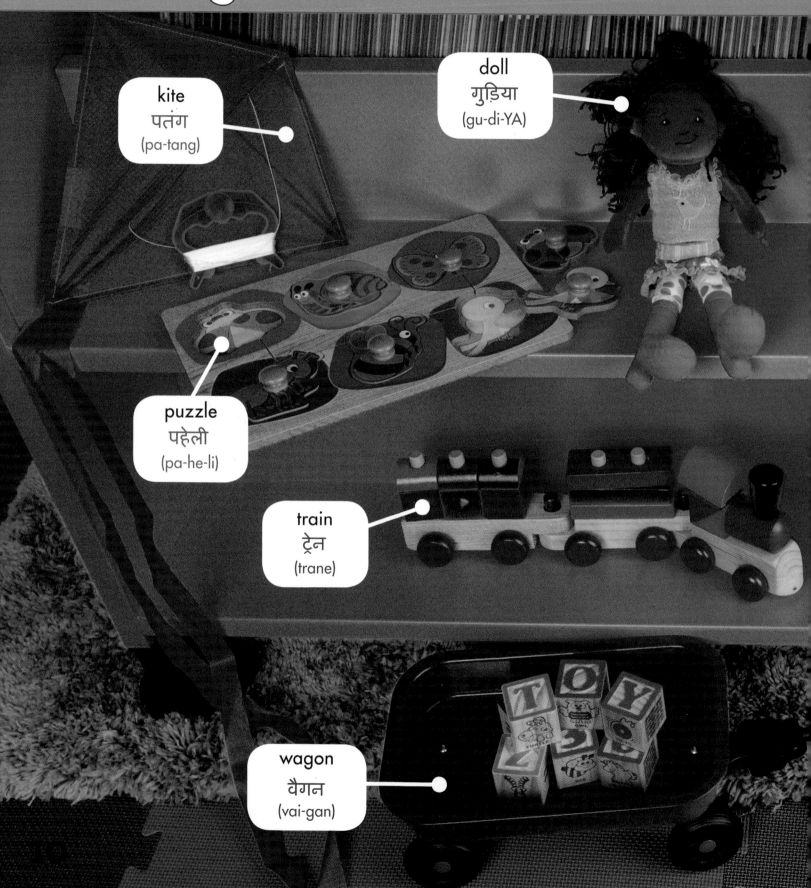

kite
पतंग
(pa-tang)

doll
गुड़िया
(gu-di-YA)

puzzle
पहेली
(pa-he-li)

train
ट्रेन
(trane)

wagon
वैगन
(vai-gan)

puppet
कठपुतली
(kath-pu-ta-li)

skateboard
स्केटबोर्ड
(SKATE-bord)

jump rope
कूदने वाली रस्सी
(koo-dane VA-LI ras-si)

ball
बॉल
(bawl)

bat
बैट
(bat)

window
खिड़की
(khi-daki)

picture
चित्र
(chi-tra)

lamp
लैंप
(lamp)

dresser
ड्रैसर
(DRESS-ur)

curtain
पर्दा
(par-DA)

blanket
कंबल
(kam-bal)

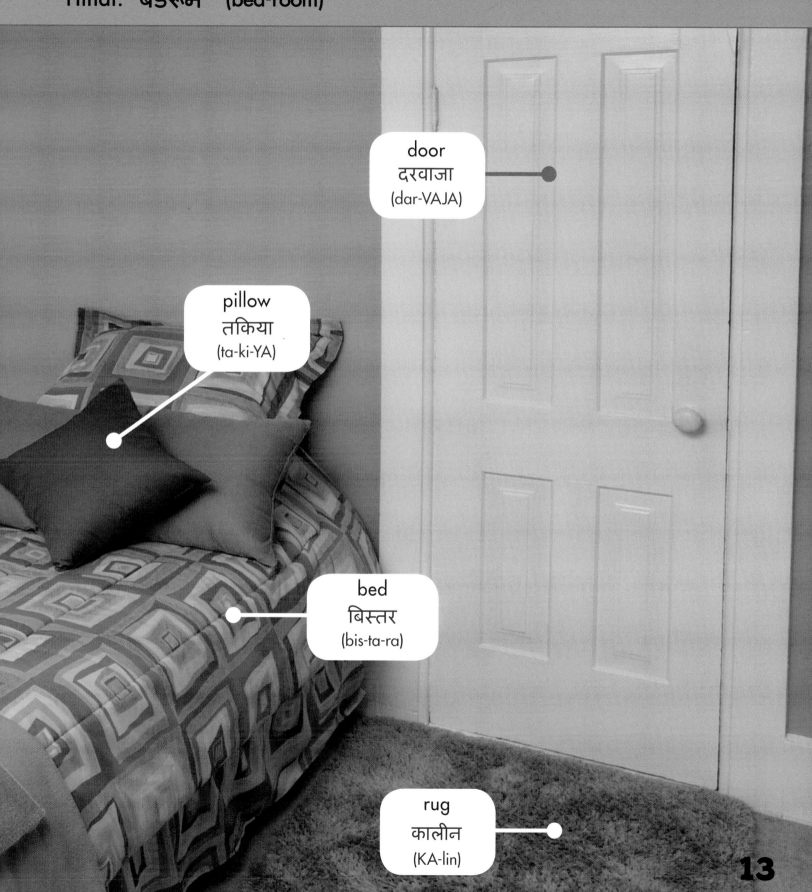

door
दरवाजा
(dar-VAJA)

pillow
तकिया
(ta-ki-YA)

bed
बिस्तर
(bis-ta-ra)

rug
कालीन
(KA-lin)

13

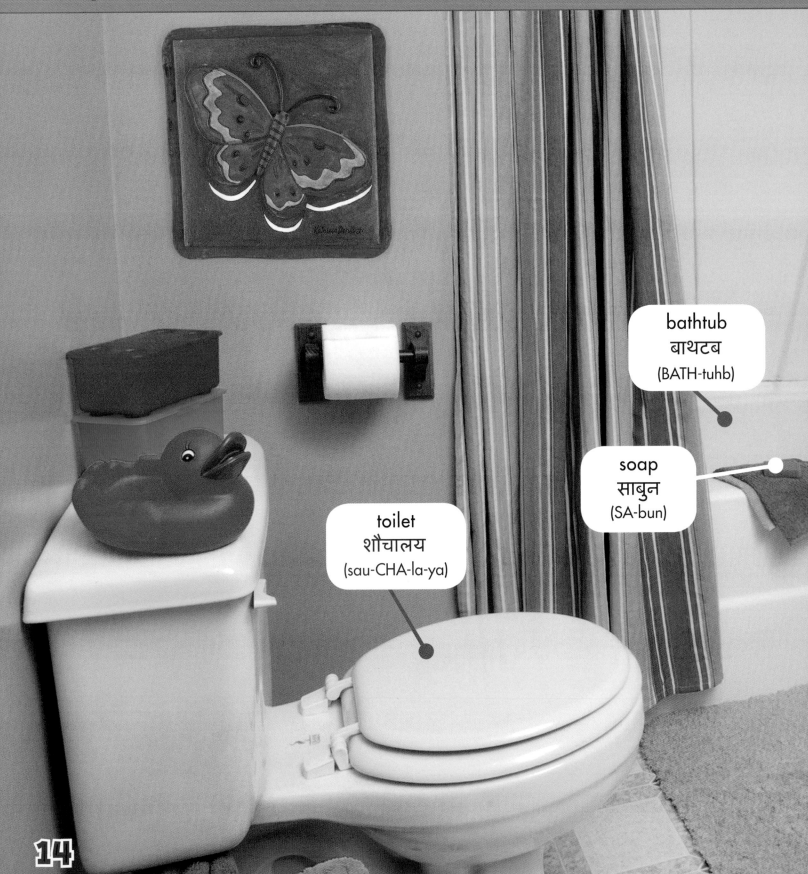

bathtub
बाथटब
(BATH-tuhb)

soap
साबुन
(SA-bun)

toilet
शौचालय
(sau-CHA-la-ya)

Hindi: बाथरूम   (bath-room)

mirror
शीशा
(shi-SHA)

toothbrush
टूथब्रश
(TOOTH-bruhsh)

toothpaste
टूथपेस्ट
(TOOTH-payst)

comb
कंघा
(kan-GHA)

sink
सिंक
(singk)

towel
तौलिया
(tau-li-YA)

brush
ब्रश
(bruhsh)

bowl
कटोरा
(ka-to-RA)

stove
स्टोव
(stohv)

pot
बर्तन
(bar-tan)

oven
ओवन
(UHV-uhn)

16

refrigerator
फ्रिज
(phrij)

knife
चाकू
(CHA-koo)

table
मेज
(mej)

spoon
चम्मच
(cham-ma-ch)

plate
प्लेट
(playt)

fork
कांटा
(KAN-ta)

17

milk
दूध
(DOO-dha)

carrot
गाजर
(GA-jar)

bread
ब्रेड
(bred)

apple
सेब
(seb)

butter
मक्खन
(mak-khan)

Butter
NET WT 4 OZ (1/4 LB) 113.4

Butter
NET W

18

egg
अंडा
(an-DA)

pea
मटर
(ma-tar)

orange
संतरा
(san-ta-RA)

sandwich
सैंडविच
(SAND-wich)

rice
चावल
(CHA-val)

tractor
ट्रैक्टर
(trai-kta-ra)

hay
भूसा
(bhoo-SA)

fence
बाड़ा
(ba-da)

farmer
किसान
(kis-AN)

sheep
भेड़
(bhed)

pig
सूअर
(su-ar)

horse
घोड़ा
(gho-DA)

barn
खलिहान
(kha-li-HAN)

cow
गाय
(gay)

chicken
चूजा
(choo-JA)

21

leaf
पत्ती
(pat-ti)

butterfly
तितली
(ti-ta-li)

flower
फूल
(phool)

shovel
बेलचा
(bel-CHA)

bird
पक्षी
(pak-shi)

worm
कीड़ा
(kee-DA)

plant
पौधा
(pau-DHA)

grass
घास
(ghas)

Edamame Green Soybean
Tohya
Glycine max

$2.99
Net Weight
15 grams

80 days
Warm season
crop – plant after
last chance of
spring frost

So high in
protein, it is
called "the meat
without bones".
Boiled, beans
are popped out
of the pod into
your mouth for
a culinary
delight!

Botanic

Chives

dirt
धूल
(dhool)

seed
बीज
(beej)

23

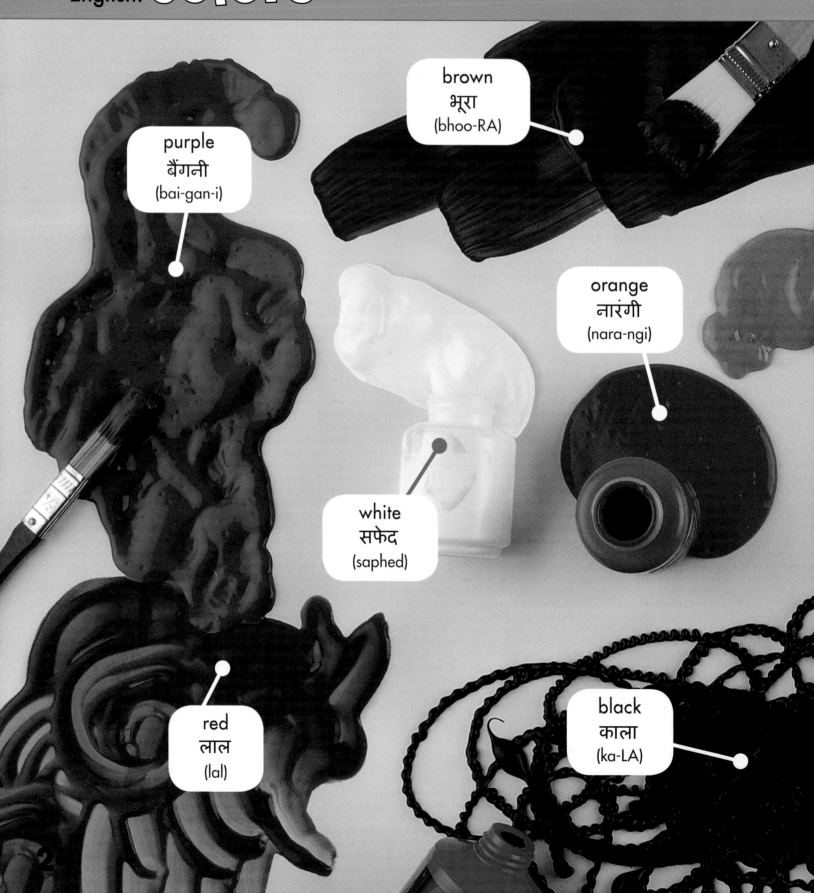

purple
बैंगनी
(bai-gan-i)

brown
भूरा
(bhoo-RA)

orange
नारंगी
(nara-ngi)

white
सफेद
(saphed)

red
लाल
(lal)

black
काला
(ka-LA)

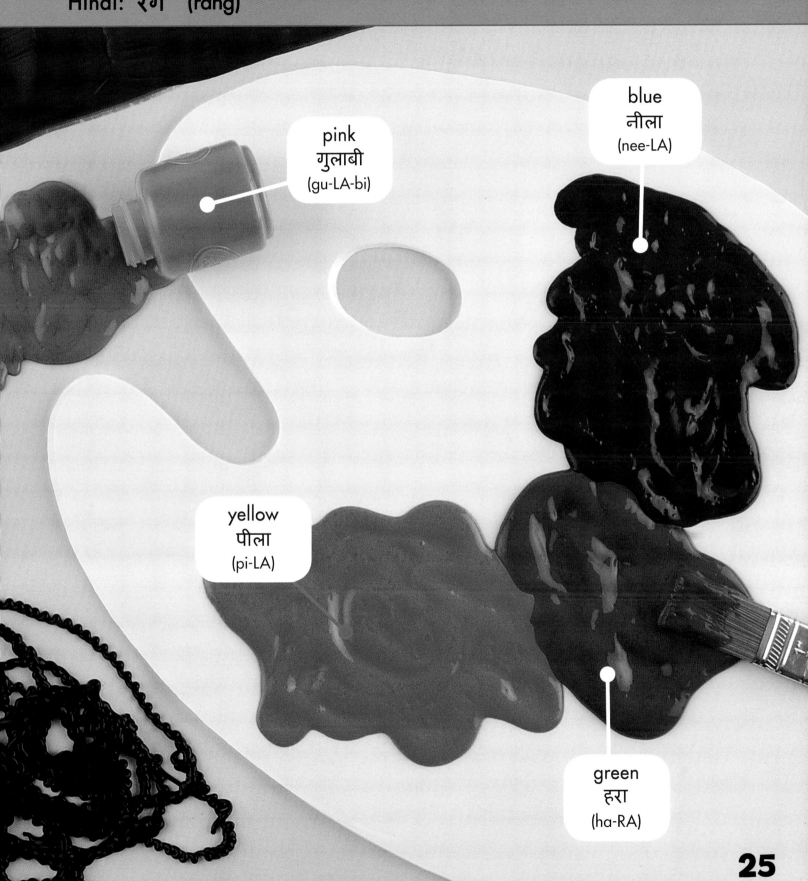

pink
गुलाबी
(gu-LA-bi)

blue
नीला
(nee-LA)

yellow
पीला
(pi-LA)

green
हरा
(ha-RA)

teacher
अध्यापिका
(ad-HYA-pika)

book
किताब
(ki-TAB)

desk
डेस्क
(desk)

pencil
पेंसिल
(PEN-suhl)

crayon
क्रेयान
(cre-YAN)

map
मानचित्र
(MAN-chi-tra)

clock
घड़ी
(gha-rhi)

computer
कंप्यूटर
(kuhm-PYOO-tur)

chair
कुर्सी
(kur-si)

paper
कागज
(KA-gaj)

traffic light
ट्रैफ़िक लाइट
(TRAF-ik LITE)

library
पुस्तकालय
(pu-sta-KA-lay)

store
स्टोर
(stor)

LIBRARY

ONE WAY

Tuesday 2:00-5:00
Thursday 2:00-6:00

bicycle
साइकिल
(sai-kil)

car
कार
(kar)

tree
पेड़
(ped)

bus
बस
(BUHSS)

park
पार्क
(park)

street
सड़क
(sa-dak)

sign
संकेत
(san-key-ta)

29

Numbers • (sank-hy-ae)

1. one • एक (ek)	6. six • छ: (chhah)
2. two • दो (do)	7. seven • सात (sat)
3. three • तीन (teen)	8. eight • आठ (atha)
4. four • चार (char)	9. nine • नौ (nau)
5. five • पाँच (panch)	10. ten • दस (das)

Useful Phrases • (upa-yo-gi vak-yan-sh)

yes • हाँ (HA)

no • नहीं (na-hi)

hello • हैलो (hel-OH)

good-bye • अलविदा (al-vi-DA)

good morning • सुप्रभात (su-pra-BHA-ta)

good night • शुभरात्रि (shu-bh-RA-tri)

please • कृपया (kri-pa-ya)

thank you • धन्यवाद (dhan-ya-VAD)

excuse me • क्षमा करें (ksha-MA ka-re)

My name is _____. • _____ मेरा नाम है. (me-RA NAM___hai)

Read More

Chandnani, Aarti. *Hindi Alphabet Writing Book.*
San Francisco: HindiGym, 2009.

Martin, Robert Stanley. *Hindi Children's Picture Dictionary.*
New York: Hippocrene Books, 2006.

Internet Sites

FactHound offers a safe, fun way to find Internet sites related to this book. All of the sites on FactHound have been researched by our staff.

Here's all you do:

Visit *www.facthound.com*

Type in this code: 9781429659673

Super-cool stuff! Check out projects, games and lots more at www.capstonekids.com

A+ Books are published by Capstone Press,
151 Good Counsel Drive, P.O. Box 669, Mankato, Minnesota 56002.
www.capstonepub.com

Books published by Capstone Press are manufactured with paper
containing at least 10 percent post-consumer waste.

Library of Congress Cataloging-in-Publication Data
Kudela, Katy R.
    My first book of Hindi words / by Katy R. Kudela.
    p. cm. — (A+ Books, Bilingual picture dictionaries.)
    Includes bibliographical references.
    Summary: "Simple text paired with themed photos invite the reader to learn to speak Hindi"—
Provided by publisher.
    ISBN 978-1-4296-5967-3 (library binding)
    ISBN 978-1-4296-6173-7 (paperback)
    1. Picture dictionaries, Hindi. 2. Picture dictionaries, English. 3. Hindi language—Dictionaries,
Juvenile—English. 4. English language—Dictionaries, Juvenile—Hindi. I. Title.
PK1936.K83 2011
491.4'3321—dc22   2010029467

Credits

Lori Bye, designer; Wanda Winch, media researcher; Eric Manske, production specialist

Photo Credits

Capstone Studio/Gary Sundermeyer, cover (pig), 20 (farmer with tractor, pig)
Capstone Studio/Karon Dubke, cover (ball, sock), 1, 3, 4–5, 6–7, 8–9, 10–11, 12–13, 14–15,
    16–17, 18–19, 22–23, 24–25, 26–27
Image Farm, back cover, 1, 2, 31, 32 (design elements)
iStockphoto/Andrew Gentry, 28 (main street)
Photodisc, cover (flower)
Shutterstock/Adrian Matthiassen, cover (butterfly); David Hughes, 20 (hay); Eric Isselee,
    20–21 (horse); hamurishi, 28 (bike); Ievgeniia Tikhonova, 21 (chickens); Jim Mills, 29
    (stop sign); Kelli Westfal, 28 (traffic light); Margo Harrison, 20 (sheep); MaxPhoto, 21
    (cow and calf); Melinda Fawver, 29 (bus); Robert Elias, 20–21 (barn, fence); Vladimir
    Mucibabic, 28–29 (city skyline)

Note to Parents, Teachers, and Librarians
Learning to speak a second language at a young age has been shown to improve overall
academic performance, boost problem-solving ability, and foster an appreciation for other
cultures. Early exposure to language skills provides a strong foundation for other subject
areas, including math and reasoning. Introducing children to a second language can help
to lay the groundwork for future academic success and cultural awareness.

Printed in the United States of America in North Mankato, Minnesota.
092010   005933CGS11